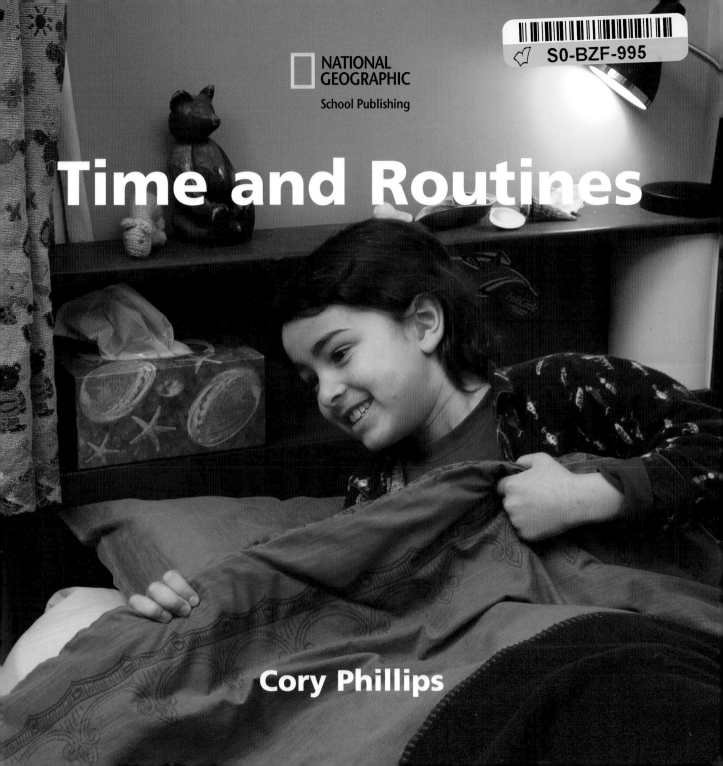

NATIONAL
GEOGRAPHIC

School Publishing

Time and Routines

Cory Phillips

PICTURE CREDITS

Illustrations by Trish Hart (4–5, 14–15).

Cover (above), 7 (above right), 8 (above center & below center), 9 (above center & below center), 10 (above left), 11 (main image), 16 (above right), Getty Images; cover (below left & below right), 1, 8 (above right & below right), 9 (above right & below right), 10 (above right), Lindsay Edwards Photography; 2, 6 (center & above right), 7 (above left & below left), 8 (above left & below left), 9 (above left & below left), 13 (above left & above right), 16 (above left & below left), Photolibrary.com; 6 (above left), Photodisc; 11 (inset), APL/Corbis; 13 (below right), Richard Hutchings/PhotoEdit, Inc.

Produced through the worldwide resources of the National Geographic Society, John M. Fahey, Jr., President and Chief Executive Officer; Gilbert M. Grosvenor, Chairman of the Board; Nina D. Hoffman, Executive Vice President and President, Books and Education Publishing Group.

PREPARED BY NATIONAL GEOGRAPHIC SCHOOL PUBLISHING

Ericka Markman, Senior Vice President and President Children's Books and Education Publishing Group; Steve Mico, Senior Vice President and Publisher; Marianne Hiland, Editorial Director; Lynnette Brent, Executive Editor; Michael Murphy and Barbara Wood, Senior Editors; Bea Jackson, Design Director; David Dumo, Art Director; Margaret Sidlowsky, Illustrations Director; Matt Wascavage, Manager of Publishing Services; Sean Philpotts, Production Manager.

MANUFACTURING AND QUALITY MANAGEMENT

Christopher A. Liedel, Chief Financial Officer; Phillip L. Schlosser, Director; Clifton M. Brown III, Manager.

BOOK DEVELOPMENT

Ibis for Kids Australia Pty Limited.

Published by the National Geographic Society
1145 17th Street, N.W.
Washington, D.C. 20036-4688

ISBN 0-7922-6061-9

Third Printing 2008
Printed in China

Contents

April

S	M	T	W	T	F	S
				1	2	3	4
5	6	7	8	9	10	11
12	13	14	15	16	17	18
19	20	21	22	23	24	25
26	27	28	29	30		

Today is **Wednesday**.
We go to music today.

4

How do you tell time?
How do you know the day of the week?

Lunch Helpers

Monday	Maria
Tuesday	Paul
Wednesday	Meg
Thursday	Lin
Friday	Chris

The Weather This Week

Monday	☀
Tuesday	☀
Wednesday	☂ ☁
Thursday	
Friday	
Saturday	
Sunday	

Telling Time

We use **clocks** and watches to tell **time**. They tell us about hours and minutes.

Every Day

Some things happen at the same time every **day**.

Pablo gets up at 7 o'clock in the morning.

Pablo comes home from school at 3 o'clock in the afternoon.

Pablo eats dinner at 5 o'clock in the evening.

Pablo goes to bed at 9 o'clock at night.

Days of the Week

A week has 7 days. Some things happen on the same day every **week**.

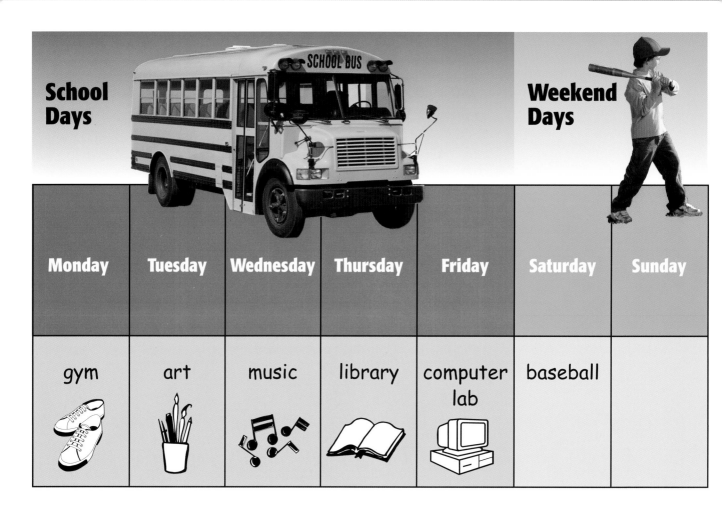

School Days					Weekend Days	
Monday	Tuesday	Wednesday	Thursday	Friday	Saturday	Sunday
gym	art	music	library	computer lab	baseball	

Monday   soccer
Tuesday   club meeting
Wednesday
Thursday   soccer
Friday   piano lesson
Saturday   school fair
Sunday   picnic

School Fair
Saturday
April 11
10 – 3
Family Fun!
Prizes!
Pony Rides!

Months of the Year

A year has 12 months. Some things happen in the same **month** every **year**.

January	February	March
April	May	June
July	August	September
October	November	December

March

Sunday	Monday	Tuesday	Wednesday	Thursday	Friday	Saturday
1	2	3	4	5	6	7
8	9	10	11 ★ Sarah's birthday	12	13	14
15	16	17	18	19	20	21 1st day of Spring
22	23 ★ Andrew's birthday	24	25	26	27	28
29	30	31				

Good Morning
8 o'clock News

8:00

Diary

14

What do you do at the same time every day?

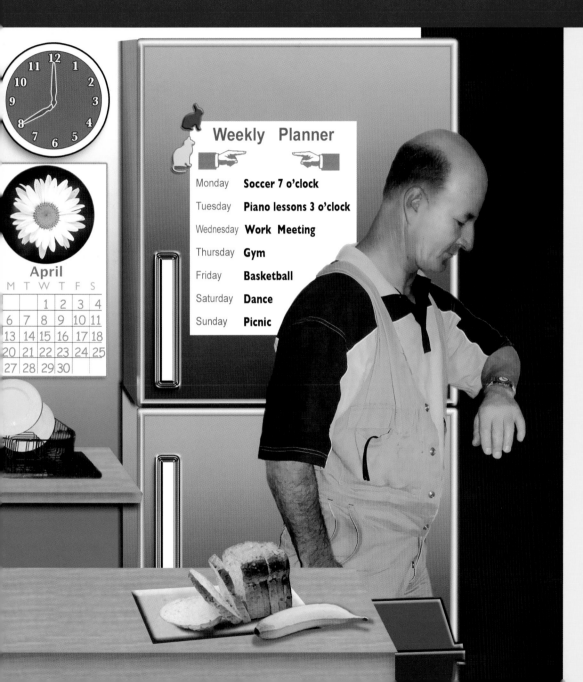

Weekly Planner

Monday	Soccer 7 o'clock
Tuesday	Piano lessons 3 o'clock
Wednesday	Work Meeting
Thursday	Gym
Friday	Basketball
Saturday	Dance
Sunday	Picnic

April

M	T	W	T	F	S
	1	2	3	4	
6	7	8	9	10	11
13	14	15	16	17	18
20	21	22	23	24	25
27	28	29	30		

day

time

clock

o'clock

week

month

year

15

Picture Glossary

calendar

clock

watch

January	February	March
April	May	June
July	August	September
October	November	December

year